TH

THE MILLENNIUM
JOKE BOOK

belongs to

Karl Rem

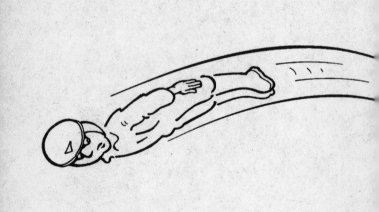

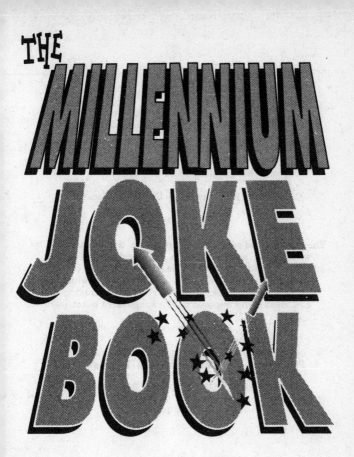

THE MILLENNIUM JOKE BOOK

Sue Mongredien

Illustrated by Raymond Turvey

RED FOX

A Red Fox Book

Published by Random House Children's Books
20 Vauxhall Bridge Road, London SW1V 2SA

A division of Random House UK Ltd
London Melbourne Sydney Auckland
Johannesburg and agencies throughout the world

Typeset by SX Composing DTP, Rayleigh, Essex
Printed and bound in Norway by AIT Trondheim AS

RANDOM HOUSE UK Limited Reg No. 954009

ISBN 0 09 940209 2

CONTENTS

THE ELEVENTH CENTURY

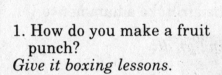

1000 A.D.

1. How do you make a fruit punch?
Give it boxing lessons.

2. Why was the surgeon working on the motorway?
It needed bypass surgery.

3. What tuba can't you play?
A tuba toothpaste.

4. Why did the chicken cross the road?
For some fowl reason.

5. What do geese eat?
Gooseberries.

6. What do hedgehogs have for lunch?
Prickled onions.

7. What lies at the bottom of the sea and
   shivers?
A *nervous wreck.*

8. Why did the girl take a hammer to
   school?
It was breaking-up day.

9. Why did the dog wear black boots?
His brown ones were at the menders.

10. Why did the apple tree cry?
*Because people were always picking on
   him.*

11. What did
    the panda
    take on
    holiday?
*Just the bear
    necessities.*

12. Did you hear about the man with jelly and sponge in one ear and a glass of sherry in the other?
He was a trifle deaf.

13. GRANNY: 'I had to get up early this morning and open the door in my nightie.'
ANNIE: 'That's a funny place to have a door, Granny!'

14. 'When my grandma went to the dentist, she had all her teeth taken out.'
'What did she say when she got home?'
'Never again! Never again!'

15. Who sleeps at the bottom of the sea?
Jack the Kipper.

1016: King Canute comes to the throne
What reptile was on the throne in 1016?
King Canewt.

17. What did King Canute get on his birthday?
A little older.

18. Why is it trendy to lose your temper?
It's all the rage.

19. Why did the priest giggle?
Mass hysteria.

20. POLICEMAN: 'We're looking for a suspect with a hearing aid.'
POLICEWOMAN: 'Wouldn't a pair of glasses be more useful?'

21. Why can't you starve at the seaside?
Because of the sand which is there.

22. What do you call one hundred strawberries lined up one behind the other?
A strawberry jam.

23. Why did the little girl stand on her head?
She was turning things over in her mind.

24. Why did the silly boy eat a pound coin?
His mum told him it was for his lunch.

25. What did the shoe say to the foot?
'You're having me on!'

26. What happens if you throw a blue hat in the Red Sea?
It gets wet.

27. What leaves footprints on the sea bed?
A sole.

28. And what's black, floats on the sea and whispers, 'Panties!'?
Refined oil.

29. What's grey and has a trunk?
A mouse going on holiday.

30. And what's brown with a trunk?
A mouse coming back from his holiday.

31. What does a deep-sea diver get paid when he works extra hours?
Undertime.

32. What's black, floats on the sea and shouts, 'Knickers!'?
Crude oil.

33. 'Doctor, Doctor – my wooden leg is giving me terrible pain!'
'How's that?'
'Every time I come home from the pub, my wife hits me over the head with it . . .'

34. Two drunks were staggering home
    one night. One looked up to the sky
    and said, 'Is that the sun or the moon?'
*'I don't know,' replied the other one. 'I
don't live around here.'*

35. What happened to the man who ate a
    lot of sugar?
He got a lump in his throat.

36. 'Doctor, Doctor – I feel half-dead!'
*Don't worry, I'll make arrangements for
    you to be buried up to your waist . . .'*

37. LISA: 'Did your watch stop when it hit the floor?'
LIZZIE: 'Well, it didn't go straight through, silly!'

38. Why is it bad to write on an empty stomach?
Because paper's much better.

39. PE TEACHER: 'Can you stand on your head?'
NICOLA: 'No, it's too high.'

40. What letters are bad for your teeth?
DK.

41. Why did the man paint himself gold?
Because he had a gilt complex.

42. Why was the patient laughing all through his operation?
Because the doctor put him in stitches.

43. 'Doctor, Doctor – I think I'm a clock!'
'Well, don't get wound up about it . . .'

44. Two fat men ran in a race.
One ran in short bursts, the other in burst shorts.

45. What do you call a cat who eats acid drops?
A sour puss.

46. Where do birds go on holiday?
The Canary Islands.

47. When should a mouse carry an umbrella?
When it's raining cats and dogs.

48. And what's worse than raining cats and dogs?
Hailing taxis.

49. What's green and smooth and goes *hith*?
A snake with a lisp.

50. What's white and fluffy and beats its chest in a cake shop?
A meringue-utang.

51. And what swings about the cake shop, yodelling?
Tarzipan.

52. Did you hear the story about the cornflake packets that had a fight?
You'll have to wait for next week – it's a serial.

53. What stays hot even if you put them in the fridge?
Chilli peppers.

54. How do you know if a sausage doesn't like being fried?
It spits at you.

55. 'What's on the telly tonight, Dad?'
'Same as ever, son – the goldfish bowl and lamp.'

56. What weighs two thousand pounds and wears a flower behind its ear?
A hippy potamus.

1057: Macbeth is killed by Malcolm III
Which raincoat was killed by Malcolm III?
Mac-beth.

58. What's yellow and black with red spots?
A leopard with measles.

59. Did you hear about the twenty-stone woman who got engaged to the twenty-five-stone man?
They plan to have a big wedding.

60. Why did the orange stop?
It ran out of juice.

61. How can you tell that coconut juice is nutty?
Because it lives in a padded cell.

62. How do you calculate the colour of plums?
With a green gauge.

63. What sort of musical instrument did ancient Britons play?
The Anglo-Saxophone.

64. How do you get a wild duck?
Buy a tame one and annoy it.

65. What has five dozen keys but never opens a door?

A piano.

1066: William the Conqueror defeats King Harold at the Battle of Hastings

What's shiny, brown and whizzes through the air?

William the Conker.

67. What was the best way to escape the Normans?

Run.

68. What do you call King Harold with an arrow through his eye?

Dead.

69. 'My brother thinks he's a chicken.

We'd take him to the doctor's, but we'd miss the eggs.'

70. What did one sole say to the other?

'Watch out, two heels are following us.'

71. Where does Tarzan get his clothes from?

A jungle sale.

72. Where does Thursday come before Wednesday?

In the dictionary.

73. What were the American gangster's last words?

'Who put that violin in my violin case?'

74. What's musical and holds thirty-six gallons of beer?

A barrel organ.

75. What song was sung when the yacht exploded?

'Pop goes the wee sail.'

76. What's the longest word in the dictionary?

Smile – because it's got a mile between the first and last letters.

77. Why is elastic one of the longest
    words in the dictionary?
Because it stretches.

78. What's the definition of a volcano?
A mountain with hiccups.

79. What's the definition of *illegal*?
A sick bird.

80. What's the definition of an
    archaeologist?
A person whose career is in ruins.

81. What's the definition of *minimum*?
A very small mother.

82. DRIVER: 'Could you
    tell me the way to
    Bath?'
POLICEMAN: 'I always
    use soap and water.'

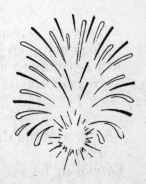

83. NEWSREADER: 'A pet shop in
   Birmingham was burgled today.
   *Police cannot find the thief because there
   aren't any leads.'*

84. NEWSREADER: 'Two prisoners escaped
   today. One is seven foot tall and the
   other is four foot six inches.
   Police are looking high and low for them.'

85. What do you get if you cross a mouse
   with an orange?
   A pipsqueak.

**1086: The Domesday Book is
   compiled**
Where do you find a list of graveyards?
The Tombsday Book.

87. MAN IN A PET SHOP: 'Do you have any
   dogs going cheap?'
PET SHOP OWNER: 'Sorry, mate – all ours
   go *woof, woof*!'

88. What's the difference between a
   duck?
One of its legs is both the same.

89. What's the difference between a well-dressed man and a tired dog?
The man wears a suit, the dog just pants.

90. What's the difference between a cup of tea and a magician?
One's a cuppa – the other's a saucer-er.

91. What did the baby sardine say when it saw the submarine?
'Look, Mum, a tin of people!'

92. What's a keycutter's favourite kind of music?
Lock 'n' roll.

93. What did Noah say when he heard the rain falling?
''Ark!'

94. How do you get rid of water on the knee?
Wear drainpipe trousers.

95. What do you call an Eskimo's cow?
An Eskimoo.

96. What goes *dot-dot-dot-croak*?
Morse toad.

97. What goes *quick-quick*?
A duck with hiccups.

98. Why couldn't the sailors play cards
on board ship?
Because the captain sat on the deck.

99. What did one angel say to the other
angel?
'Halo, there!'

100. What does Dracula write on his
Christmas cards?
'Best vicious of the season.'

THE TWELFTH CENTURY

1100 A.D.

1100: Henry I comes to the throne
What was Henry I after he was four days old?
Five days old.

2. Why did the zombie decide to stay in his coffin?
Because he felt rotten.

3. What's white, furry and smells of peppermint?
A polo bear.

4. 'Doctor, Doctor – I keep thinking I'm a goat.'
'How long have you had this feeling?'
'Ever since I was a kid.'

5. How do you make a Mexican chilli?
Take him to the North Pole.

6. What coat do you put on only when it's wet?
A coat of paint.

7. Did you hear about the sheepdog trials?
Three of the dogs were found guilty.

8. What bet can never be won?
The alphabet.

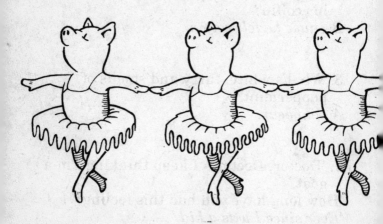

9. What happened to the man who stole a
   calendar?
He got twelve months.

10. How did Moses part the Red Sea?
With a seasaw.

11. What food sings?
A soup opera.

12. What's a pig's favourite ballet?
Swine Lake.

13. MAN IN CHEMIST: 'Have you got any
    rat poison?'
CHEMIST: 'No, sorry. Have you tried
    Boots?'
MAN: 'I want to poison them, not kick
    them to death!'

14. And what's a squirrel's favourite
    ballet?
The Nutcracker.

15. Did you hear about the artist's model
    who died when the painter threw his
    paintbrush at her?
She had an art attack.

16. Why did the bald man take up
    jogging?
To get some fresh 'air.

17. MAN: 'Six packets of mothballs,
    please.'
CHEMIST: 'But I sold you six packets
    yesterday!'
MAN: 'I know, but my aim's not very good
    and I keep missing them.'

18. Little pigeon in the sky,
Dropping things from way up high.
Farmer Giles wipes his eye,
Thanking God that cows don't fly!

19. What do you call a blind buck?
No-eye deer.

20. What's the difference
between elephants and
boiled potatoes?
You can't mash elephants.

21. What did the nun say when she went
over the zebra crossing?
'Now you see me, now you don't.'

22. What do you get if you cross a sheet
of glass with indigestion?
A pane in the guts.

23. What are two-tonne raindrops called?
Heavy showers.

24. What do you get if you cross a
    sheepdog with a vegetable?
A collieflower.

25. Why were two flies playing football in
    a saucer?
They were practising for the cup.

26. What would you do if you got a
    button stuck up your nose?
Breathe through those four little holes.

27. What illness do retired
    pilots get?
Flu.

28. How do footballers stay
    cool?
They have a lot of fans.

29. What did one candle say
    to the other?
'You're getting on my wick.'

30. TEACHER: 'When was Rome built?'
KATIE: 'At night, sir.'
TEACHER: 'What makes you say that?'
KATIE: 'Well, I heard that Rome wasn't built in a day.'

31. What happened when the hammer was invented?
It made a great impression.

32. Why do they put telephone wires so high?
To keep up the conversation.

33. PORTER: 'Can I carry your bag, sir?'
MR BROWN: 'No, let her walk.'

34. Where would you find the Andes?
At the end of your wristies.

1135: Matilda wages civil war for the English throne
HENRY II: 'Mummy, Mummy, why are your hands so lovely and soft?'
QUEEN MATILDA: 'Because I make the servants do all the housework.'

36. **What did Queen Matilda say on the first day of January 1136?**
'Happy New Year.'

37. KAREN: 'I was shipwrecked in the ocean and had to live on a tin of baked beans for a week.'
DARREN: 'You're lucky you didn't fall off.'

38. **What's the noblest dog of all?**
A hot dog, because it feeds the hand that bites it.

39. **Why are flowers lazy?**
They are always found in beds.

40. MUM: 'Who told you you were a good book-keeper?'
JOE: 'The librarian.'

41. What made the garden laugh?
The hoe-hoe-hoe.

42. What did the polar bear have for lunch?
Iceburgers.

43. What keys are furry?
Monkeys.

44. What do gorillas sing at Christmas time?
'Jungle bells, jungle bells . . .'

45. What did the skunk say when the wind changed direction?
'Ah, it's all coming back to me now.'

46. 'Doctor, Doctor – I feel like a dog.'
'Sit down and tell me all about it.'
'I can't, I'm not allowed on the furniture . . .'

47. 'Doctor, Doctor, I keep thinking I'm a dustbin.'
'Don't talk rubbish . . .'

1148: Crusaders attempt to recapture the Holy Land

What steps would you take if the crusaders were after you?

Big ones.

49. DOCTOR: 'Do you talk in your sleep?'
TEACHER: 'No, I talk in other people's.'

50. When is a brown dog not a brown dog?

When it's a greyhound.

51. When is a door not a door?

When it's ajar.

52. When is it bad luck to have a black cat following you?
When you're a mouse.

53. Two eggs were boiling in a pan. One said, 'It's hot in here, isn't it?'
The other said, 'Wait till you get out, they bash your head in!'

54. Why are the letters *N* and *O* important?
You can't get on *without them.*

55. What is white, yellow and goes at 100 mph across the country?
A train driver's egg sandwich.

56. How can you stop food going bad?
Eat it.

57. What do you call five bottles of cola?
A pop group.

58. What's tall and wobbly and stands in the middle of Paris?
The Trifle Tower.

59. What runs around the forest making the other animals yawn?
A wild bore.

60. What's a crocodile's favourite game?
Snap.

61. What do you get if you cross a zebra with a pig?
Striped sausages.

62. What animal has two humps and is found at the North Pole?
A lost camel.

63. Why can't leopards escape from the zoo?
Because they're always spotted.

64. Why did the woman keep her blonde wig on the lamp?
Because it was a light shade.

65. Where are kings and queens usually crowned?
On the head.

66. How do you swim a hundred metres in two seconds?
Swim over a waterfall.

67. CONDEMNED MAN: 'Can I have one last request?'
EXECUTIONER: 'Very well.'
CONDEMNED MAN: 'I'd like to sing a song before I die.'
EXECUTIONER: 'Go ahead.'
CONDEMNED MAN: *'Ten thousand green bottles hanging on a wall . . .'*

68. What pets make the most noise?
Trumpets.

69. What's the best present you can give someone?
A drum takes a lot of beating.

1170: Thomas Becket is murdered in Canterbury Cathedral
What lay dead and full of water in Canterbury Cathedral in 1170?
Thomas à Bucket.

71. What is at the end of everything?
The letter G.

72. What begins with *T*, ends with *T* and has *T* in it?
A teapot.

73. How do the police give chase under water?
They use a squid car.

74. Why did the policewoman climb the tree?
She was in the Special Branch.

75. BEN: 'When I grow up, I'm going to be a policeman and follow in my father's footsteps.'
LEN: 'I didn't know your dad was a policeman.'
BEN: 'He's not, he's a burglar.'

76. What kind of ears does a train have?
Engineers.

77. Who gets a lot of kicks out of his job?
A footballer.

78. CAPTAIN: 'Why didn't you stop the
    ball?'
GOALIE: 'What do you think the net's for?'

79. What's the difference between a train
    driver and a teacher?
*One minds the train, the other trains the
    mind.*

80. Where do Volkswagens go when they
    get old and battered?
The Old Volks' home.

81. What do you get if you cross a pig
    with a motorway?
A road hog.

82. Who was the fastest runner in
    history?
Adam. He was first in the human race.

83. What is a big game hunter?
A man who gets lost on his way to the FA Cup Final.

84. I occur once in every minute, twice in every moment, but not once in a hundred thousand years. What am I?
The letter M.

85. What did the big bell say to the little bell?
Give me a ring sometime.

86. Which Christmas carol is popular in the desert?
'O camel ye faithful . . .'

87. How does Jack Frost get to work?
By icicle.

88. What's white and goes up?
A silly snowflake.

89. What runs around all day and lies
about at night with its tongue hanging
out?
A pair of trainers.

90. Where do fairies go shopping?
British Gnome Stores.

**1191: Richard the Lionheart leads
the third Crusade**
Why did Richard the Lionheart cut the
legs off his bed?
He wanted to lie low for a while.

92. What do all women look for, but hope never to find?
Holes in their tights.

93. What gets wetter the more it dries?
A towel.

1194: Richard the Lionheart is crowned King on his return to England
ANTIQUE DEALER: 'This is Richard the Lionheart's skull.'
COLLECTOR: 'How can it be? It's far too small.'
ANTIQUE DEALER: 'Yes, well, this was his skull when he was a little boy.'

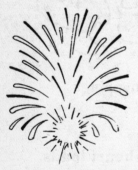

95. What kind of shoes do you make from banana skins?
Slippers.

96. What dress does everyone have, but nobody wears?
An address.

97. What happens when you slip on thin ice?
Your bottom gets thaw.

98. When is a boat like a heap of snow?
When it's adrift.

99. What trees are always sad?
Pine trees.

100. What do you get if you cross a witch with a snowstorm?
A cold spell.

THE THIRTEENTH CENTURY

1200 A.D.

1. What do you get if you cross an elephant with a shark?
Swimming trunks with sharp teeth.

2. Have you heard about the plastic surgeon?
He sat by the fire and melted.

3. FAT LADY: 'Could you see me across the road, constable?'
POLICEMAN: 'I could see you a mile away, ma'am!'

4. What stands still and goes?
A clock.

5. How can you stop your dog barking in the back garden?
Put him in the front garden.

6. TEACHER: 'If I gave you three white rabbits and five grey rabbits, how many rabbits would you have?'
SAM: 'Nine, miss.'
TEACHER: 'Nine?'
SAM: 'Yes, miss, we've got another one at home.'

7. What's worse than finding a maggot in an apple?
Finding half a maggot.

8. When are sheep like ink?
When they're in a pen.

9. Why did the farmer drive a steamroller over his field?
He wanted to grow mashed potato.

10. What would you get if you set fire to a nun?
Holy smoke.

11. What did the tablecloth say to the table?
'Don't move, I've got you covered.'

12. What made the Tower of Pisa lean?
A strict low-calorie diet.

13. If a buttercup's yellow, what colour is a hiccup?
Burple.

14. What steals soap from the bath?
Robber ducks.

1215: The Magna Carta is signed at Runnymede

Where did King John sign the Magna Carta?

At the bottom.

16. What would you give a nervous elephant?

Trunkquillisers.

17. What do gnus read in the mornings?

Gnus-papers.

18. How do cows keep up to date with current affairs?

They watch the Nine o'clock Moos.

19. Why is a sofa like a roast chicken?

They're both full of stuffing.

20. Where are whales weighed?

At a whale-weigh station.

21. Which birds spend all their time in church?

Birds of prey.

22. How do you make a cheese roll?
Push it down a hill.

23. What do you call a man who can't
stop buying mats?
A rug addict.

24. 'Doctor, Doctor – what can I do about
my flat feet?'
'Use a foot pump . . .'

25. TEACHER: 'I hope I didn't see you
looking at someone else's exam paper,
Sally.'
SALLY: 'I hope so too, miss.'

26. What do you call a judge with no
fingers?
Justice Thumbs.

27. MR JONES: 'When I left my last place,
the landlady cried.'
LANDLADY: 'Well, I shan't. I ask for rent
in advance.'

28. SARAH: 'I've decided to let my hair grow.'
SIMON: 'How can you stop it?'

29. What yard has four feet?
A back yard with a dog in it.

30. What's the best way to prevent diseases caused by biting insects?
Don't bite any.

31. Did you hear about what happened to the flea circus?
A dog came along and stole the show.

32. Why do lions have fur coats?
They'd look silly in anoraks.

33. Why did the robot go mad?
He had a screw loose.

34. Why are storytellers weird creatures?
Because tales come out of their heads.

35. How do you stop yourself dying?
Stay in the living room.

36. Why did the girl keep her piano in a
    deepfreeze?
Because she liked to play it cool.

37. What is green, hairy and takes
    aspirins?
A gooseberry with a headache.

38. Why aren't there any aspirins in the
    jungle?
*Because the parrots eat 'em all
(paracetamol).*

39. If milk comes from a cow, where does
    wine come from?
A wine-oceros.

40. What happened to the manager of the
    biscuit factory?
He went crackers.

41. 'Doctor, Doctor – I feel like a cricket
    ball.'
'How's that?'
'Don't you start!'

42. What's black, crazy and sits in a tree?
A raven lunatic.

43. Why was the bit of black tarmac scared of the bit of green tarmac?
Because he was a cycle path (psychopath).

44. What do a dentist and a farmer have in common?
They both deal in acres (achers).

45. When do streets get greasy?
When the rain is dripping.

46. VICAR: 'Do you say your prayers before dinner, Cathy?'
CATHY: 'No, my mum's a good cook.'

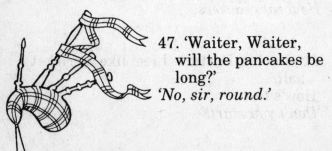

47. 'Waiter, Waiter, will the pancakes be long?'
'No, sir, round.'

48. 'Waiter, Waiter, what soup is this?'
'It's bean soup.'
*'It might have been once, I want to know
   what it is now!'*

49. 'Waiter, Waiter, there's a fly in my
     soup!'
*'Don't worry, sir, the spider in
the salad will get it.'*

50. Why can you never win at
    cards in the jungle?
There are too many cheetahs.

51. What did the jack say to the car?
'Can I give you a lift?'

52. Why did Little Bo-Peep lose her
    sheep?
She had a crook with her.

53. BOY: 'Dad, I don't need a bike for
    Christmas any more.'
DAD: 'Why not?'
BOY: 'I found one behind the wardrobe.'

54. What spins and does not stop?
The world.

55. What happens to tyres when they get old?
They are retired.

56. And what happens to bikes when they get old?
They are recycled.

57. Who was the first person to wear a shell suit?
Humpty Dumpty.

58. What did the dentist say when she saw something bad?
'Oh, sugar!'

59. What did the gas meter say to the pound coin?
'Glad you dropped in, I was just going out.'

60. DOCTOR: 'Have you had this before?'
MAN: 'Yes, I have.'
DOCTOR: 'Well, you've got it again.'

61. What do you call a cheeky cabbage?
A fresh vegetable.

62. What did the big firecracker say to
the little firecracker?
My pop's bigger than your pop.

63. 'Doctor, Doctor – my hair's coming
out. Can you give me something to
keep it in?'
'Certainly, here's a paper bag . . .'

**1264: Henry III's incompetent rule
provokes the Barons' war**
HENRY III: 'I can lift an elephant with one
hand.'
QUEEN ELEANOR: 'I've never seen a one-
handed elephant!'

65. Why is an elephant big, grey and
wrinkly?
*Because if he was small, white and
round, he'd be an aspirin.*

66. JASON: 'Do you notice any change in me?'
MUM: 'No, why?'
JASON: 'I've just swallowed a five-pence coin.'

67. What did the first mind-reader say to the second mind-reader?
'You're all right, how am I?'

68. Why do golfers take an extra pair of trousers with them?
In case they get a hole in one.

69. WOMAN: 'Did you just save my son from drowning?'
MAN: 'Yes, I did.'
WOMAN: 'Well, where's his cap?'

70. What did the judge say to the dentist?
'Do you swear to pull the tooth, the whole tooth and nothing but the tooth?'

71. 'Who's that at the door?'
'The Invisible Man.'
'Tell him I can't see him.'

72. TOM: 'Where are you going, Mum?'
MUM: 'To the doctor's, I don't like the look
of your sister.'
TOM: 'I'll come with you. I don't like the
look of her either.'

73. SANDY: 'My granny lived to be ninety-
nine and never used glasses.'
ANDY: 'Well, lots of people drink straight
from the bottle.'

74. What knocks you senseless every
night but doesn't hurt you?
Sleep.

75. Why is an island like the letter *T*?
It's in the middle of water.

76. When did the first two vowels
   appear?
Before U *and* I *were born.*

77. Take away my first letter, take away
   my second letter – in fact, take away
   all my letters and I'm still the same.
   What am I?
A postman.

78. Why do Eskimos eat whale meat and
   blubber?
*You'd blubber too if you had to eat whale
   meat.*

79. What did the gas say to the coal?
'What kind of fuel am I?'

80. DAD: 'I never told lies when
   I was a child.'
CINDY: 'So when did you begin?'

81. What three letters frighten off a thief?

'I.C.U.'

82. What's the most unfortunate letter of the alphabet?

The letter U *– whenever there's trouble, you'll always find* U *in the middle of it.*

83. POLICEMAN: 'I'm sorry, son, but you need a permit to fish here.'

ALAN: 'Thanks, but I'm doing OK with a worm.'

1284: Edward I conquers Wales
What did Edward I do when he burped?
He issued a royal pardon.

85. What do you call a flying policeman?
A heli-copper.

86. MAN: 'A return ticket, please.'
TICKET OFFICER: 'Where to?'
MAN: 'Why, back here, of course!'

87. PASSENGER: 'How long will the next train be?'
PORTER: 'Six carriages, sir.'

88. Why couldn't the bicycle stand up?
Because it was tyred.

89. Why did the man drive his car into a lake?
He was trying to dip his headlights.

90. Why are the goods on board a ship like petrol?
They both make a car go.

91. What has twenty-two legs and two wings, but can't fly?
A football team.

92. FOOTBALLER: 'I have a good idea to improve the team.'
MANAGER: 'Good, are you leaving?'

93. Which team's footballers have never met each other before?
Queen's Park Strangers.

94. Why did the silly man jump out of the window?
To try out his new jump suit.

95. What wears shoes but has no feet?
A pavement.

96. What's the best way to cover a cushion?
Sit on it.

1297: William Wallace defeats the English at Stirling
Who went out clubbing after victory at the battle of Stirling Bridge?
Raveheart.

98. Where do you find giant snails?
On the end of giants' fingers.

99. Where do insects live?
Crawley.

100. What do you get if you cross an elephant with a box of laxatives?
Out of the way.

THE FOURTEENTH CENTURY

1300 A.D.

1. What do you call a camel with three humps?
Humphrey.

2. DINER: 'There's something wrong with these eggs!'
WAITRESS: 'Don't blame me, I only laid the table.'

3. DINER: 'Why has this lobster only got one claw?'
WAITER: 'I think it must have been in a fight, sir.'
DINER: 'Well, could you bring me the winner?'

4. TIM: 'I hear egg shampoo is good for your hair.'
JIM: 'Yes, but how do you get a chicken to lay an egg on your head?'

5. How do fleas get from place to place?
By itch-hiking.

6. Why shouldn't you tell a secret to a pig?
Because they're squealers.

7. What do you get if you cross a galaxy with a toad?
Star Warts.

8. 'There's a man at the door with a wooden leg.'
'Tell him to hop it.'

9. What do you call a sheep with a machine gun?
Lambo.

10. What goes *zzub, zzub*?
A bee flying backwards.

11. NURSE: 'I bet your wife misses you a lot.'
PATIENT: 'No, she's got an excellent aim. That's why I'm here.'

12. Did you hear about the dentist who married the manicurist?
After a month they were fighting tooth and nail.

13. What do angels dance to?
Soul music.

1314: Robert the Bruce defeats the English at Bannockburn
Why did Robert the Bruce go to the barber and get his head shaved?
Because he couldn't stand his hair any longer.

15. Which pirate had the biggest hat?
The one with the biggest head.

16. Why didn't the sea horse believe what the sardine said?
Because it sounded fishy.

17. Why did the crab blush?
Because the sea weed.

18. How can you tell if there's an elephant in your fridge?
The door won't close.

19. What question can never be answered by *yes*?
'Are you asleep?'

20. SILLY BILLY: 'Is it raining outside?'
CLEVER TREVOR: 'Well, it doesn't often rain inside.'

21. When is a monkey like a flower?
When it's a chimp-pansy.

22. What has twelve legs, six ears and one eye?
Three blind mice and half a kipper.

23. What is the cheapest time to telephone friends in Australia?
When they're out.

24. How long does it take a candle to burn?
About one wick.

25. What kind of clothing could you make from tea bags?
A baggy T-shirt.

26. 'Doctor, Doctor – what can I do about my broken leg?'
'Limp . . .'

27. How can you tell the time by candles?
By the candles-tick.

28. WAYNE: 'May I hold your hand?'
JANE: 'No thanks, it isn't heavy.'

29. What insect can fly under water?
A mosquito in a submarine.

30. Why is the sky cleaner in New York than it is in London?
Because there are more skyscrapers.

31. Why did the frankfurter turn red?
It saw the salad dressing.

32. What do you call two turnips in love?
Swedehearts.

33. What do you do with a wombat?
Play wom of course!

34. Where would you find a cockney with pimples?
'Ackney.

35. What makes people shy?
Coconuts.

36. WAITER: 'Would you like your coffee black?'
DINER: 'What other colours do you have?'

1337: The Hundred Years' War breaks out
What do you get if you cross the Sleeping Beauty with a battle, and the year 1337?
The Hundred Years' Snore.

38. How can you get eggs without keeping hens?
Keep ducks instead.

39. Why are tall people more lazy than short people?
Because they lie longer in bed.

40. What do you get if you cross a cocoa bean with an elk?
A chocolate moose.

41. What did the bell say when it fell in the river?
I'm wringing wet.

42. What job do hippies do?
They hold your leggies on.

43. What do you feed little pixies?
Elf-raising flour.

44. Why did the man wear a lot of clothes to paint his house?
Because the tin said, 'Put on three coats'.

45. Why wasn't Cinderella any good at
    football?
Because she had a pumpkin for a coach.

46. 'If I had fifty pounds in one pocket
    and one hundred pounds in the other
    pocket, what would I have?'
'Someone else's trousers on.'

47. 'Waiter, Waiter, there's a footprint in
    my pudding!'
'Well, you did tell me to step on it.'

48. 'Waiter, Waiter, there's a twig in my
    soup.'
*'Just a moment, madam, I'll call the
    branch manager.'*

**1349: The Black Death sweeps
    through Europe and Asia**
What smells disgusting, has two legs and
    flies?
A victim of the Black Death.

50. Who was the father of the Black
    Prince?
Old King Coal.

51. **What did one lift say to the other lift?**
'I think I'm coming down with something.'

52. **What's yellow, brown and hairy?**
Cheese on toast on the carpet.

53. **What happened to the boy who slept with his head under the pillow?**
The tooth fairy took his head away.

54. **What do you get if you cross rabbits with leeks?**
Bunions.

55. MAN IN RESTAURANT: 'Will you join me in a bowl of soup?'
WOMAN: 'Do you think there's room for both of us?'

56. **What did they do when the Forth Bridge collapsed?**
Built a fifth one.

57. **Can an orange box?**
No, but a tomato can.

58. What do you call a
man who shaves
twenty times a day?
A barber.

59. Why did the man ask
for alphabet soup?
*So he could read while
he was eating.*

60. What goes *Ha Ha Bonk?*
A man laughing his head off.

61. What do policemen have in their
sandwiches?
Truncheon meat.

62. What happens if you dial 666?
A policeman comes along upside down.

63. Where do policemen live?
999 Letsbe Avenue.

64. What's a twack?
Something a twain runs on.

65. Which driver never commits a traffic offence?
A screwdriver.

66. Why can't a steam engine sit down?
Because it has a tender behind.

67. What's the hardest thing about learning to skateboard?
The pavement.

68. What ring is square?
A boxing ring.

69. What do miners play in the pit?
Mineopoly.

70. What does a winner lose in a race?
Their breath.

71. Why are farmers cruel?
Because they pull corn by its ears.

72. MR SMITH: 'I went home last night to
find my son in our lounge in front of a
blazing fire.'
MR EDWARDS: 'What's wrong with that?'
MR SMITH: 'We haven't got a fireplace.'

73. Where do cows go on holiday?
Moo York.

74. What bird is always out of breath?
A puffin.

75. MRS JONES: 'My son's a conductor.'
MRS BROWN: 'Musical or on the buses?'
MRS JONES: 'Electrical. He was struck by
lightning.'

76. What's round and purple and bad at
cooking?
Alfred the Grape.

77. What is a cold war?
A snowball fight.

78. MUM: 'We're having Grandma for Christmas dinner this year.'
BILLIE: 'I hope she's not as tough as last year's turkey!'

79. Why was the farmer cross?
Someone trod on his corn.

EEF IF OF MUF

80. What is tall and goes *eef, if, of, muf*?
A backward giant.

1381: The Peasants' Revolt

ROYAL BUTLER: 'The peasants are revolting, sir.'

RICHARD II: 'Tell me something I don't know!'

82. 'My dad was a Pole.'
'North or South?'

83. What smells most in any garden?
Your nose.

84. What water won't freeze?
Boiling water.

85. How do you service a pogo stick?
Give it a spring clean.

86. Why shouldn't you tell a joke whilst ice skating?
The ice might crack up.

87. Why did the boy's mother knit him three socks for his birthday?
Because he'd grown another foot.

88. What do you get if you cross egg white with gunpowder?
A boom-meringue.

89. Who is never hungry at Christmas?
A turkey – it's always stuffed.

90. What do you call a crate of ducks?
A box of quackers.

91. Why did the turkey cross the road?
To prove he wasn't chicken.

92. Why did the fish blush?
Because it saw the ocean's bottom.

93. Why do gorillas have big nostrils?
Have you seen the size of their fingers?

94. Where do tadpoles change into frogs?
In a croakroom.

95. What kind of crisps can fly?
Plane crisps.

96. What's the best cure for dandruff?
Baldness.

97. Who serves spirits on an aeroplane?
The air ghostess.

98. What do witches like reading in the
newspaper?
Their horrorscopes.

99. Why didn't the old skeleton want to
go to the party?
His heart wasn't in it.

100. Why are ghosts so bad at lying?
You can see right through them.

THE FIFTEENTH CENTURY

1400 A.D.

1. How do you make antifreeze?
Hide her nightie.

2. 'What do you get if you cross a turkey
   with an octopus?'
*'I don't know, but everyone gets a leg
   each.'*

3. 'What do geese watch on
   television?
Duckumentaries.

4. BILLY: 'My dad can jump higher than a
   house!'
SAM: 'Oh yeah?'
BILLY: 'Yeah, houses can't jump.'

5. What happened when the abominable snowman bought a curry?
He melted.

6. Where do geologists go in their spare time?
Rock concerts.

7. Why did the witch put her broomstick in the washing machine?
She wanted a clean sweep.

8. Where do ghosts enjoy swimming?
In the Dead Sea.

9. 'Mummy, Mummy – I don't want to go
   to America!'
'Shut up, and keep swimming!'

10. Why do pirates carry swords?
Because swords can't walk.

11. Where do lobsters keep their money?
In a sand bank.

12. What do you do if you find a vampire
    in your bed?
Sleep somewhere else.

13. How many skunks does it take to
    make a house smell?
Just a phew.

14. What can a whole orange do that half
    an orange can't?
Look round.

15. Why did the farmer call his horse
    Blacksmith?
*Because it kept trying to make a bolt for
    the door.*

16. Why should you never listen to a
    pirate in bed?
Because he's lying.

17. What's a horse's favourite game?
Stable tennis.

18. BRUCE: 'Help, a shark's just bitten my
    leg off!'
SHEILA: 'Which one?'
BRUCE: 'I don't know – they all look the
    same to me!'

19. How can you tell if your grandpa has
    a glass eye?
It usually comes out in conversation.

20. What's the hottest part of
    a man's face?
His sideburns.

21. What is green, curly and shy?
Lettuce alone.

22. Why is the letter *F* like a cow's tail?
Because it's always on the end of beef.

23. Why did the Mexican push his wife
off a cliff?
Tequila.

24. What happened to the bricklayer who
fell into the cement mixer?
He became a very hard man.

25. What was the turtle doing on the M4?
About one mile an hour.

26. What did the lumberjack do before
Christmas?
He went on a chopping spree.

27. What is black and white
and red all over?
An embarrassed zebra.

28. Why did the ant elope?
Nobody gnu.

29. Why did the Romans build straight roads?
So the Britons couldn't hide round corners.

1430: Joan of Arc is burned at the stake
What do you get if you cross Joan of Arc with a boomerang?
A terrible burning smell you can't get rid of.

31. How do chickens communicate?
Fowl language.

32. What sort of tiles can't be stuck on walls?
Reptiles.

33. What do you get if you cross an owl with a pair of your dad's socks?
A bird that stinks but doesn't give a hoot.

34. What would happen if pigs could fly?
The price of bacon would go up.

**35. What did the mouse say when
it broke its two front teeth?**
'Hard cheese.'

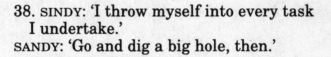

36. Where do spiders play football?
Webley.

**37. What did the hamburger say
to the tomato?**
'That's enough of your sauce!'

38. SINDY: 'I throw myself into every task
I undertake.'
SANDY: 'Go and dig a big hole, then.'

39. How do you hire a horse?
Put four bricks under him.

**40. What did the launch pad say to the
rocket?**
'Clear off, you're fired.'

41. Where do cows go when they want a night out?

The moooovies.

42. What do you get if you cross a man with a goat?

Someone who is always butting into other people's affairs.

43. What happened to the snake who had a cold?

She adder viper nose.

44. 'Waiter, Waiter, have you got frogs' legs?'

'No, I always walk this way.'

45. 'Waiter, Waiter, have you got frogs' legs?'

'Certainly, madam.'

'Then leap over the counter and get me a drink.'

46. 'Waiter, Waiter, do you serve crabs?'

'Sit down, sir, we serve anyone.'

47. WAITER: 'How did you find your steak, madam?'
DINER: 'Quite by accident. I moved a few peas and there it was.'

48. What's the best butter in the world?
A goat.

49. What always walks with its head down?
The nail in your shoe.

50. What always goes to bed with its shoes on?
A horse.

51. What goes up and down but never moves?
Stairs.

52. What sort of robbery is the easiest?
A safe robbery.

53. What does the Invisible Man call his mum and dad?
Transparents.

54. Why did the frog jump in the pond when it started to rain?
So he wouldn't get wet.

1455: The Wars of the Roses break out
What do you call a fight in a chocolate factory?
The War of the Roses.

56. How did Henry VI dress on a cold day?
Quickly.

57. What part of the army can babies join?
The infantry.

58. What goes black, white, black, white, black, white?
A puffin rolling down a hill.

59. And what's black and white and laughs?
The puffin who pushed the other one down the hill.

60. What did the electrician's wife say when he arrived home late?
'Wire you insulate?'

61. What's the most shocking city in the world?
Electri-city.

62. What did the north wind say to the east wind?
Let's play draughts.

63. What sits at the bottom of the sea and makes the other fish offers they can't refuse?
The Cod Father.

64. What horse can't you ride?
A clotheshorse.

65. What do you give a pony with a cold?
Cough stirrup.

66. What is green, has two legs and a trunk?
A seasick tourist.

67. TEACHER: 'How do you spell *inconsequentially*?'
PUPIL: 'Always the wrong way.'

68. TEACHER: 'Jackie, you missed school yesterday, didn't you?
JACKIE: 'No, miss, not at all.'

69. 'Did you hear the joke about the bodysnatchers?
I'd better not tell you – you might get carried away.'

70. What has a neck but cannot swallow?
A bottle.

71. What does a cashier do in a police station?
He counts coppers.

72. Why are policemen strong?
Because they can hold up traffic.

73. Why did the policeman cry?
Because he couldn't take his panda to bed.

74. What did Big Chief Running Water call his baby?
Little Drip.

75. How do you start a jelly race?
Say, 'Get set'.

76. How do you start a teddy race?
'Ready, teddy, go.'

77. How do you start a flea race?
'One, two, flea, go.'

78. What's cowardly, thin and full of noodles?
Chicken soup.

79. Why did the man hit the dentist?
Because he got on his nerves.

80. What do you call a cow eating grass?
A lawn-mooer.

81. How did the
human cannonball lose his job?
He got fired.

82. What did the bull sing to the cow?
'When I fall in love... it will be for heifer.'

83. 'Who's that at the door?'
'A woman with a pram.'
'Tell her to push off.'

84. What race is never run?
A swimming race.

85. What do you call a bull asleep on the ground?
A bulldozer.

86. Where does a sick ship go?
To the dock.

87. What was written on the metal monster's gravestone?
Rust In Peace.

88. Why did the man put birdseed in his trainers?
Because he had pigeon toes.

89. 'Was Dracula ever married?'
'No, he was a bat-chiller.'

90. What does Dracula like for dessert?
Nectarines.

91. What do you get if you cross a football team with an ice cream?
Aston Vanilla.

1492: Christopher Columbus discovers the New World

Which bus sailed the ocean in 1492?
Columbus.

93. Which pantomime is set in a chemist's?
Puss in Boots.

94. What did Cinderella say when the chemist lost her photos?
'Someday my prints will come.'

95. Who shouted 'knickers' at the big bad wolf?
Little Rude Riding Hood.

96. Why did the tightrope-walker ask for his bankbook?
He wanted to check his balance.

97. Why did Nellie the elephant leave the circus?
She was tired of working for peanuts.

98. MUM: 'Why are you crying?'
LISA: 'Dad hit his thumb with a hammer.'
MUM: 'Knowing you, I'm surprised you
didn't laugh.'
LISA: 'That's the trouble – I did.'

99. Did you hear about the man who
went to a New Year's Eve party
dressed as a bone?
A dog ate him in the hall.

100. Did you hear that joke about the
poker game?
Never mind – it's no big deal.

THE SIXTEENTH CENTURY

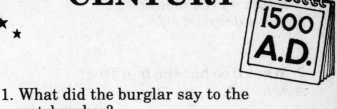

1. What did the burglar say to the watchmaker?
'Sorry to have taken so much of your valuable time.'

2. What prize did the woman who invented doorknockers win?
The Nobel Prize.

3. What's the difference between a fisherman and a naughty schoolboy?
One baits his hooks, the other hates his books.

4. What are assets?
Little donkeys.

5. What's higher than an Admiral?
An Admiral's hat.

6. What happened when the lazy pirate
   rested on the plank?
He soon dropped off.

7. What tree has the best food?
A pantry.

8. What did the big candle say to the
   little candle?
'I'm going out tonight.'

1509: Henry VIII becomes King of England

What was Henry VIII's middle name?
The.

10. What did Henry VIII get for
    Christmas?
Fat.

11. When is a ship not a ship?
When it turns into a harbour.

12. Did you hear the joke about the skunk?
Don't bother, it stinks.

13. How do you stop a skunk smelling?
Put a peg on its nose.

14. When is a sailor like a plank of wood?
When he's aboard.

15. How do you stop a bull charging?
Take away its credit card.

16. How do you make a slow tortoise fast?
Don't feed him for a fortnight.

17. When does an elephant weigh as much as a mouse?
When the scales are broken.

18. What type of lights were on Noah's ark?
Floodlights.

19. And where did Noah keep the bees?
In the ark hives.

20. Why did the ocean roar?
Wouldn't you if you had crabs on your bottom?

21. PET SHOP OWNER: 'That's a very clever bird, sir. If you pull the string on its left leg it sings *Rule Britannia*, and if you pull the string on its right leg, it sings *God Save the Queen*.'
CUSTOMER: 'What happens if I pull both strings at once?'
PARROT: 'I fall off my perch, you idiot!'

22. 'Did you hear about the new Member of Parliament who took his seat in the House of Commons?
The police arrested him and made him take it back.'

23. What's yellow and stupid?
Thick custard.

24. A girl in a sweet shop is 1.5 metres tall and wears size five shoes. What does she weigh?
Sweets.

25. 'Mum, will my measles be better next week?'
'I couldn't say – I hate to make rash promises.'

26. 'My brother gets a warm reception wherever he goes.'
'He must be popular.'
'No, he's a fireman.'

27. Have you heard the one about the man who bought a paper shop?
It blew away.

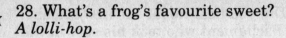

28. What's a frog's favourite sweet?
A lolli-hop.

29. What's huge, icy and tastes delicious?
A glacier mint.

30. 'Doctor, Doctor – I keep thinking I'm a bird.'
'Well, perch yourself there and I'll tweet you in a minute . . .'

31. What did the burglar say to the lady of the house when she caught him stealing her silver?
'I am at your service, madam.'

32. 'Doctor, Doctor – I keep thinking I'm a strawberry.'
'Hmm, you're really in a jam, aren't you?'

1533: Henry VIII marries Anne Boleyn

What did Anne Boleyn's mother say when her daughter confessed she loved Henry VIII?
'That man's not worth losing your head over.'

34. Have you heard the one about the man who stood in front of a mirror with his eyes closed?
He wanted to see what he looked like asleep.

35. I have five noses, six mouths and seven ears. What am I?
Ugly.

1536: Anne Boleyn is beheaded

Why did Henry VIII have so many wives?
He liked to chop and change.

37. Think of a number between one and
    twenty. Double it, subtract sixteen,
    add seven, multiply by five, close your
    eyes . . .
Dark, isn't it?

38. Why did the cookie cry?
*Because its mother had been a wafer so
    long.*

39. Why did the dog chase its tail?
To make both ends meet.

40. What's the difference between a dog
    and a flea?
*The dog can have a flea but the flea can't
    have a dog.*

41. What goes *woof, woof, tick, tick*?
A watchdog.

42. When is a red-headed idiot like a
    biscuit?
When he's a ginger nut.

43. What's a lawyer's favourite pudding?
Sue-it.

44. What do pixies have for tea?
Fairy cakes.

1545: The *Mary Rose* sinks
TEACHER: 'Give me a sentence containing
  the words *Mary Rose.*'
SILLY SAM: 'Mary sat on a pin. Mary rose
  up quickly.'

46. What has eight feet and can sing?
A quartet.

**47. Have you heard the one about the
  man who always wore sunglasses?**
He took a dim view of things.

48. Why are dolphins clever?
They swim around in schools.

**49. What's the best thing to give as a
  parting gift?**
A comb.

50. What gets bigger the more you take
    away from it?
A hole.

51. What is a blooming nuisance?
A weed.

52. What can go up a drainpipe down,
    but can't go down a drainpipe up?
An umbrella.

53. Spell a hungry horse in four letters.
M.T.G.G.

54. What is horse sense?
Just stable thinking.

55. Why did the teacher wear dark
    glasses?
Because her class was so bright.

56. What is always coming but never
    arrives?
Tomorrow.

57. Why is an old car like a baby?
It never goes anywhere without a rattle.

**58. PATIENT: 'Tell me the truth, doctor –
is it serious?'**
DOCTOR: 'Well, I wouldn't start watching
any new serials if I were you.'

**1559: Elizabeth I establishes the
Church of England**
Why did Elizabeth I go to bed?
The bed wouldn't go to her.

**60. What's yellow and goes *slam, slam,
slam, slam*?**
A four-door banana.

61. What's a good way of putting on weight?
Eat a peach, swallow the centre and you've gained a stone.

62. How do you spell a word with more than a hundred letters in it?
P-O-S-T-O-F-F-I-C-E.

63. What's purple and hums?
An electric plum.

1564: William Shakespeare is born
Why was Shakespeare able to write so well?
Where there's a will, there's a way.

65. Did Shakespeare snore?
Only when he was asleep.

66. What did Juliet say when she met Romeo on the balcony?
'Couldn't you get seats in the stalls?'

67. TEACHER: 'If Shakespeare were alive today, he'd still be an admirable man.'
PUPIL: 'Yes, he would. He'd be over 400 years old.'

68. What should you do if a dog swallows your pen?
Use a pencil.

69. Newsflash: A lorry-load of wigs has been stolen in Manchester.
Police are combing the area.

70. POSTMAN: 'You've put too many stamps on this letter, miss.'
DIANA: 'Does that mean it'll go too far?'

71. Shall I tell you the joke about the high wall?
I'd better not, you'd never get over it.

72. Where did Humpty Dumpty put his hat?
Humpty dumped 'is 'at on the wall.

73. Humpty Dumpty sat on the wall
Humpty Dumpty had a great fall
All the king's horses
And all the king's men
Said, 'Scrambled eggs for dinner again!'

74. FARM HAND: 'What a lovely colour
that cow is.'
FARMER: 'It's a Jersey.'
FARM HAND: 'Is it really? I thought it was
its skin.'

75. What did the ram say to his
girlfriend?
I love ewe.

76. What do you get if you cross a sheep
with a kangaroo?
A jumper with a pocket.

77. How can you hammer in nails
without hitting your thumb?
Get someone else to hold the nail.

78. 'Doctor, Doctor – every bone in my
body aches.'
'Just be thankful you're not a herring . . .'

79. MRS BROWN: 'I want you to keep that
dog out of the
house – it's full of
fleas.'
MR BROWN: 'Rover,
don't go in the
house, it's full of
fleas!'

**1580: Francis
Drake completes his round-the-
world voyage**
Why couldn't Francis Drake handle the
Captain's log?
He kept getting splinters in his fingers.

81. Doctor: 'You must take things quietly
from now on.'
Patient: 'I do, I'm a cat burglar.'

82. What do you call a man who's good at
gardening?
Pete.

83. What do you call a man with a
wooden head?
Edward.

84. What do you call a man with three
    wooden heads?
Edward Woodward.

85. Where do musicians often live?
In A flat.

86. Passenger: 'Conductor, do you stop at
    the Savoy Hotel?'
Conductor: 'What, on my salary? You
must be joking!'

87. When is a car like a sausage?
When it's an old banger.

**1588: The Spanish Armada is
    defeated by English fleets**
What did the ocean do when it saw the
    Spanish Armada?
Nothing, it just gave a little wave.

89. What musical instrument does a
    skeleton play?
The trom-bone.

90. How can you say 'rabbit' without using the letter R?
'Bunny.'

91. What do you see from the top of the Eiffel Tower?
An eyeful.

92. Why did the girl put sugar under her pillow?
She wanted sweet dreams.

93. What part of a car causes the most accidents?
The nut that holds the steering wheel.

94. Who is the meanest man in the world?
The one who found a sling and broke his arm to put in it.

95. Why did the mother flea cry?
Because all her children had gone to the dogs.

96. What has four eyes but cannot see?
The Mississippi.

97. What colours would you paint the sun and the wind?
The sun rose and the wind blue.

98. Who carries a broom in a football team?
The sweeper.

99. Why wasn't the little boy hurt when he sat on the pin?
It was a safety pin.

100. What happens to a frog when it gets cross.
It becomes hopping mad.

THE SEVENTEENTH CENTURY

1600 A.D.

1. FARMER: 'My hen lays square eggs –
   and can speak, too!'
   POSTMAN: 'That's amazing – what does it
   say?'
   FARMER: '"Ouch."'

2. How does an elephant get down from a
   tree?
   He sits on a leaf and waits for autumn.

3. MUM: 'Andy and Mark, stop fighting – I
   want you to learn to give and take.'
   ANDY: 'I already know – I took his sweets
   and gave him a punch.'

4. 'How come you're only wearing one
   glove? Did you lose one?'
   No, I found one!'

1605: Conspirators hatch the Gunpowder Plot

Who had a bushy tail and was hung for trying to blow up Parliament?
Guy Fox.

6. Who invented gunpowder?
A woman who wanted rifles to look pretty.

7. RECEPTIONIST: 'The new doctor's so funny, he'll have you in stitches.'
PATIENT: 'I hope not, I only came in for a checkup.'

8. What did the oil painting say to the wall?
First they framed me, then they hung me.

9. What do you call a good-looking friendly monster?
A failure.

10. There were two kings in bed. Which one wore the pyjamas?
Mr King. His wife was wearing a nightie.

11. What do vampires have every
    morning at 10.30?
A coffin break.

12. Why are pirates so strong?
Because they hold up ships.

13. What's the fastest fish?
A motorpike.

14. What Spanish musical instrument
    helps you fish?
A castanet.

15. BOB: 'What's your dog's name?'
RYAN: 'I don't know – he won't tell me.'

16. 'My gran's parrot is a bit of a boozer.'
'Really?'
'Yeah, it's drinking so much it's laying Scotch eggs!'

17. Why did the pig cross the road?
It was the chicken's day off.

18. OLD LADY: 'This budgie you sold me hasn't said a single word, and you promised it would repeat everything it heard.'
SHOPKEEPER: 'So it would, only it's stone deaf.'

19. BAZ: 'I've just got a bottle of champagne for my wife.'
DAZ: 'Blimey, what a swap!'

1620: The Pilgrim Fathers reach America
On which ship did the first insects sail to America?
The Mayfly.

21. If April showers bring May flowers,
   what do Mayflowers bring?
Pilgrims.

22. When do elephants have eight feet?
When there are two of them.

23. Which takes less time to get ready for
   a holiday, an elephant or a rooster?
A rooster – he only takes his comb.

24. 'Doctor, Doctor – everyone keeps
   being rude to me.'
'Get out of here, you silly fool!'

25. FIRST TONSIL: 'What are you getting
   all dressed up for?'
SECOND TONSIL: 'The doctor's taking me
   out tonight.'

26. 'Doctor, Doctor – I keep thinking
   there's two of me.'
'One at a time, please.'

27. WOMAN: 'I bought a carpet which was in mint condition.'
NEIGHBOUR: 'What do you mean?'
WOMAN: 'There was a hole in the middle of it.'

28. WOMAN: 'You remind me of the sea.'
MAN: 'Because I'm wild, reckless and romantic?'
WOMAN: 'No, because you make me sick.'

29. JUDGE: 'Have you been up before me before?'
THIEF: 'I don't know, what time do you get up?'

30. 'Mum, does God use our bathroom?'
'What do you mean?'
'Because every morning, Dad bangs on the door and shouts, "Oh God, are you still in there?"'

31. Why do doctors and nurses wear masks?
So if they make a mistake, no one knows who did it.

32. GRANNY: 'It's raining cats and dogs today.'
ANNIE: 'I know, I've just stepped in a poodle.'

33. 'Why is it that every time the doorbell rings, my dog goes into a corner?'
'Because he's a boxer.'

34. What noise does a cat make going down the M1?
Meeeeoooooowwwwww!

35. 'I've lost my rabbit.'
'Why don't you put a note in the shop window?'
'Don't be daft – he can't read!'

36. Why are cooks cruel?
Because they whip cream, beat eggs and batter fish.

37. Two ears of corn ran up to the top of a hill. What were they when they got there?
Puffed wheat.

38. How do you make an apple puff?
Chase it round the garden.

39. What do jelly babies wear on their feet?
Gum boots.

40. What's the most dangerous cake?
Attila the Bun.

41. What's the only business you can see through?
Window cleaning.

42. What can fall on water
without getting wet?
A shadow.

43. What's got teeth but can't
bite?
A comb.

44. What's the best system of book-
keeping?
Never lend them.

45. What do you call a building with lots
of storeys?
A library.

46. 'What is frozen water?' 'Ice.'
'What is frozen milk?' 'Ice cream.'
'What is frozen tea?' 'Iced tea.'
'What is frozen ink?' 'Iced ink.'
'Well, take a bath, then!'

47. DAD: 'Do you think the teacher likes
you?'
MARK: 'Yes, she keeps putting kisses by
my sums.'

48. SARAH: 'Would you punish a pupil for something she hadn't done?'
TEACHER: 'Of course not.'
SARAH: 'Good, I haven't done my homework.'

1649: Charles I is beheaded

FIRST KNAVE: 'What did King Charles say when he heard he was going to be beheaded?'
SECOND KNAVE: 'Do you want me to leave out all the swear words?'
FIRST KNAVE: 'Yes.'
SECOND KNAVE: 'He didn't say a thing.'

50. DOCTOR: 'The best time to take a bath is just before retiring.'
MR POWELL: 'So I don't have to have another bath until I'm sixty-five?!'

51. What sits in the fruit bowl and shouts for help?
A damson in distress.

52. What drink do you give an injured lemon?
Lemon-aid.

53. What did the traffic warden have in his sandwiches?
Traffic jam.

54. Which bird can lift the heaviest weights?
A crane.

55. What letter is a bird?
The letter J.

56. And which pies are birds?
Magpies.

57. CHEMIST: 'Certainly, sir, we do make life-size enlargements of photographs.'
MAN: 'Good, here's a photograph of Buckingham Palace.'

58. DAD: 'I don't like this photo of me, it doesn't do me justice.'
MUM: 'It's not justice you want, it's mercy.'

59. MUM: 'I'm not myself tonight.'
DAD: 'Yes, I thought I noticed an
   improvement.'

60. Why are dumplings unlucky?
They're always getting into a stew.

61. What do you get if you cross a whale
   with a duckling?
Moby Duck.

62. 'Waiter, Waiter, this
   milk is weak.'
*'Well, the cow got caught
   in the rain.'*

63. JUDGE: 'Guilty. Take
   ten days in prison or a
   £500 fine.'
PRISONER: 'I'll have the £500.'

64. Do you feel like a cup of coffee?
'Of course not – do I look like one?'

65. Why did the parents call their baby
    Coffee?
Because she kept them awake all night.

**1666: The Great Fire of London
    breaks out**
Where was Charles II when the Great
    Fire of London went out?
In the dark.

67. 'What's the weather like?'
'I don't know – it's so foggy I can't see.'

68. 'Mum, we're pretending to be
    elephants at the zoo. Will you help us?'
'Of course, love. What do you want me to
    do?'
*'You can be the lady that feeds them
    buns.'*

69. Why did the lady mop up her spilt tea
    with a piece of cake?
It was sponge cake.

70. MAN: 'Will I be able to read when I
get these glasses?'
OPTICIAN: 'Certainly, sir.'
MAN: 'That's funny, I couldn't before!'

71. 'Doctor, Doctor – I feel like a pin.'
'I see your point.'

72. How does a sheep keep warm in
winter?
Central bleating.

73. Where does a lamb go when it needs
a haircut?
To the baa-baa shop.

74. Why does a rabbit have a shiny nose?
*Because its powder puff is at the other
end.*

75. How do you catch a squirrel?
Climb up a tree and act like a nut.

76. What did the stag say to his children?
'Hurry up, deers.'

77. What do you call high-rise flats for pigs?
Sty scrapers.

78. Why is an elephant in a kitchen like a house on fire?
The sooner you put it out, the better.

79. What happened to the pig who wanted to be a Shakespearean actor?
He ended up as Hamlet.

80. Why can't a man's head be twelve inches wide?
Because if it was it'd be a foot.

81. Who did Dracula marry?
The girl necks door.

82. What animal do you look like when you have a bath?
A little bear.

83. SUE: 'What's the difference between a rhinoceros, a lemon and a tube of glue?'
MARTIN: 'I don't know.'
SUE: 'Well, you can squeeze a lemon but you can't squeeze a rhinoceros.'
MARTIN: 'What about the tube of glue?'
SUE: 'I knew that's where you'd get stuck.'

84. KATE: 'My dog goes for a tramp in the woods every morning.'
CHRIS: 'Does your dog enjoy it?'
KATE: 'Yes, but the tramp's getting a bit fed up with it.'

1685: Johann Sebastian Bach is born
Why did the man call his dog Johann Sebastian?
Because of its Bach.

86. What did the ghost say to his son?
Spook only when you're spooken to.

87. DOCTOR: 'You must take four teaspoonfuls of this medicine before every meal.'
PATIENT: 'I can't.'
DOCTOR: 'Why not?'
PATIENT: 'I've only got three teaspoons.'

88. What do you call a clumsy doctor?
A medicine dropper.

89. What is the difference between ammonia and pneumonia?
One comes in bottles, the other comes in chests.

90. What has four fingers and a thumb but isn't a hand?
A glove.

91. What do you do if your dog swallows a book?
Take the words right out of his mouth.

92. What kind of car does an electrician drive?
A Voltswagen.

93. What is a polygon?
A dead parrot.

94. Shall I tell you the joke about the empty house?
There's nothing in it.

95. Why are artists never short of
    money?
Because they can always draw a cheque.

96. What is a miserable person's
    favourite game?
Moanopoly.

97. In what ball can you carry your
    shopping?
In a basketball.

98. Why was the unemployed doctor
    angry?
Because he had no patients.

99. What is always on
    at the cinema?
The roof.

100. What is another
     name for a butcher's
     boy?
A chop assistant.

THE EIGHTEENTH CENTURY

1700 A.D.

1. What's the cure for water on the brain?
A tap on the head.

2. TEACHER: 'Can you play the piano?'
DIM JIM: 'I don't know, I've never tried.'

3. What trees do fingers and thumbs grow on?
Palm trees.

4. How do you define agony?
A one-armed man with an itchy bum hanging from a cliff top.

5. What is brought to the table and cut, but never eaten?
A pack of cards.

6. If a man had fifteen cows and all but nine died, how many would he have left?
Nine.

7. Why is your heart like a policeman?
Because it follows a regular beat.

8. What is the craziest clock?
A cuckoo clock.

9. How do you make a witch scratch?
Take away the letter W.

10. Which pirate had the warmest bottom?
Long John Silver.

11. And which pirate had a parrot that shouted, 'Pieces of four!'?
Short John Silver.

12. What happened to the ship that sank in shark-infested waters?
It returned with a skeleton crew.

13. MARTIN: 'I can't stand the sun, it's driving me mad!'
STEVE: 'Well, why don't you try the *Guardian*?'

14. What's a thief's favourite musical instrument?
A lute.

15. What's the most dangerous flower?
A dandelion.

16. What kind of cat lives in the ocean?
An octopus.

17. What do you call a baby crab?
A little nipper.

18. What weighs more – a pound of lead or a pound of feathers?
Neither – they both weigh the same.

19. What type of house weighs the least?
A lighthouse.

20. What can run but can't walk?
Water.

21. Where would a man post a letter in
    his sleep?
In a pillow box.

22. Where do elves go to get fit?
Elf farms.

23. What's a vampire's favourite tourist
    spot?
The Vampire State Building.

24. What kind of boats do vampires like?
Blood vessels.

 25. Which is the fastest – heat
    or cold?
*Heat, because you can catch
    cold.*

26. How does a fireplace feel when you fill it with coal?
Grate-full.

27. What's the difference between a wizard and the letters M, A, K, E, S.
One makes spells and the other spells makes.

28. 'Doctor, Doctor – I keep seeing little black spots in front of my eyes.'
'Have you seen a doctor before?'
'No, just little black spots . . .'

29. Why are fishmongers so mean?
Because their job makes them sell fish.

30. What's the best way to catch a fish?
Get someone to throw one at you.

31. How many weeks belong to a year?
Forty-six. The rest are Lent.

32. How do you use an Egyptian doorbell?
Toot-and-come-in.

33. How does an intruder get into the house?
Intruder window.

34. Do mountains have ears?
Yes, they have mountaineers.

35. Why do elephants have big ears?
Noddy wouldn't pay the ransom.

36. What is there more of, the less you see?
Darkness.

37. What do you get when you cross an ocean with a comedian?
Waves of laughter.

38. Can you name three inventions that have helped man get up in the world?
The elevator, the escalator and the alarm clock.

39. A barrel of beer fell on a man. Why wasn't he hurt?
It was light ale.

40. 'Shall I tell you the joke about the pencil?'
'No, there's no point to it.'

41. 'Shall I tell you the joke about the bed?'
'No, it hasn't been made yet.'

42. What's the difference between a sailor and a shopaholic?
One goes to sail the seas, the other goes to see the sales.

43. What's the difference between a plane and a tree?
One leaves its shed, the other sheds its leaves.

44. What's the difference between a thief and a church bell?
One steals from the people and the other peals from the steeple.

1745: Bonnie Prince Charlie leads the Jacobite Rebellion
What type of hat did Bonnie Prince Charlie wear when it was raining?
A wet one.

46. What's the difference between a mad king and a street?
One tosses crowns and the other crosses towns.

47. ELLIE: 'I found a horseshoe today. What do you think it means?'
FIONA: 'Maybe the horse decided to wear socks.'

48. What is the longest night of the year?
A fortnight.

49. TEACHER: 'Chris, how can you prove the world is round?'
CHRIS: 'I never said it was, miss.'

50. TEACHER: 'You should have been here at nine o'clock, Charlie.'
CHARLIE: 'Why, what happened?'

51. What's orange and comes out of the ground at 90 mph?
A jet-propelled carrot.

52. Which vegetable should you pick to go with jacket potatoes?
Button mushrooms.

53. What's the difference between a mouldy lettuce and a dismal song?
One's a bad salad, the other's a sad ballad.

54. What did the baby bird say when it found an orange in the nest?
'Look at the orange marmalade!'

55. What kind of bird do you find down a coal mine?
A mynah bird.

56. What do you get if you throw a piano down a coal mine?
A Flat Minor.

57. When is a goose like a car?
When it honks.

58. What do birds eat for breakfast?
Tweet-a-bix and shredded tweet.

59. Who was Scotland's most famous Jewish poet?
Rabbi Burns.

60. DAN: 'My uncle's so rich, he owns a newspaper.'
DI: 'So what? Newspapers are only thirty pence!'

61. HEADMISTRESS: 'Do you think teenagers should wear lipstick?'
TEACHER: 'Only girl teenagers.'

62. Who is the boss of the hankies?
The hankie chief.

63. Why is getting up at three in the morning like a pig's tail?
It's twirly (too early).

64. DAD: 'My shaving brush is all hard and sticky!'
LAD: 'It was all right when I painted my bike with it yesterday . . .'

65. Did you hear about the well-behaved little boy? Every time he was good, his dad gave him twenty pence and a pat on the head.
By the time he was ten, he had £896 and a flat head.

66. Where does a swallow live?
In a throat.

67. What are sideburns?
What you get when your electric blanket is too hot.

68. TOM: 'Why are your hands shaking?'
SAM: 'They're pleased to see each other.'

69. 'Did you hear about the little boy with the turned-up nose?'
'Every time he breathed he blew his cap off.'

1770: Captain Cook discovers Australia
Which vegetable did Captain Cook ban on board HMS *Endeavour*?
Leeks.

71. TEACHER: 'If Captain Cook made five trips around the world and was killed on one of them, which one was it?'
BOB: 'You know I'm no good at history, sir.'

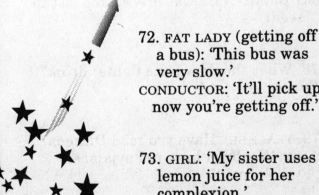

72. FAT LADY (getting off a bus): 'This bus was very slow.'
CONDUCTOR: 'It'll pick up now you're getting off.'

73. GIRL: 'My sister uses lemon juice for her complexion.'
FRIEND: 'No wonder she always looks so sour.'

74. DAD: 'Eat your spinach, Jack, it'll put colour in your cheeks.'
JACK: 'But Dad, I don't want green cheeks!'

75. What does a thirsty foot do?
Puts on tap shoes.

76. What did the finger say to the thumb?
'People will say we're in glove.'

77. POLICEMAN: 'Didn't you see the 30 mph sign?'
MOTORIST: 'No, I was driving too fast to see it.'

78. What should a prize fighter drink?
Punch.

79. TEACHER: 'Have you read Dickens?'
GARY: 'No, but I have red pyjamas.'

80. MUM: 'I've just come back from the
    beauty parlour.'
    DAD: 'Closed, was it?'

81. What did the pig say when the man
    grabbed him by the tail?
    'This is the end of me.'

82. What did the beaver say to the tree?
    'It was nice gnawing you.'

83. What can travel around the world,
    yet stay in one corner?
    A postage stamp.

84. Where do tadpoles go when they lose their tails?
To a retail shop.

85. What do you call a frog spy?
A croak and dagger agent.

86. What do you get if you cross a frog and a soft drink?
Croak-a-Cola.

87. 'Doctor, Doctor – I feel like a bridge!'
'What's come over you, man?'
'Well, so far, two cars, three lorries and a bus . . .'

88. Why did the tap dancer have to retire?
He kept falling in the sink.

1789: George Washington becomes the first president of America
Who was the cleanest American president?
George Washington.

90. Why do gardeners hate weeds?
Because if you give them an inch, they'll take a yard.

91. What causes a flood?
A river that gets too big for its bridges.

92. How can you leave a room with two legs and return with six?
Bring a chair with you.

93. What is a blood count?
Count Dracula.

94. MICK: 'My teacher shouted at me because I didn't know where the Great Wall of China was.'
MUM: 'Well, remember where you put things next time!'

95. Why did the baby pig eat so much?
To make a hog of himself.

96. What rises up in the morning and
waves all day?
A flag.

97. Did you hear about the florist who
had two children?
*One was a budding genius, the other was
a blooming idiot.*

98. Why do you always find what you've
lost in the last place you look?
*Because when you've found it, you stop
looking.*

99. Why is a fish shop crowded?
Because the fish fillet.

100. What's the best thing for water on
the knee?
Wearing pumps.

THE NINETEENTH CENTURY

1800 A.D.

1. What kind of fish is useful on ice?
A skate.

2. Who invented the first fireplace?
Alfred the Grate.

3. Where are elephants found?
They're so big they never get lost.

4. What's the hardest part
   about learning to climb the
   rigging?
The deck.

1805: Nelson dies at the Battle of Trafalgar

Where did Napoleon keep his armies?
Up his sleevies.

6. What was Nelson's little brother called?
Half-Nelson.

7. What did Nelson do when he lost a hand?
Went to the second-hand shop.

8. Why did Nelson wear a three-cornered hat?
To fit his three-cornered head.

9. How do you get a shellfish up a cliff?
Oyster up.

10. What did the envelope say when the woman licked it?
It just shut up.

11. What's green and goes *boing, boing*?
A spring cabbage.

12. What training do you need to be a litter collector?
None, you just pick it up as you go along.

13. What did one eye say to the other?
There's something between us that smells.

14. What did the little rabbit want to do when he grew up?
Join the hare force.

1815: Napoleon is defeated at the Battle of Waterloo
'One of my ancestors fell at Waterloo.'
'Really?'
'Yeah – he was pushed off platform five.'

16. What happened when the Duke of Wellington gave the order to fire at Waterloo?
Napoleon was Blownapart.

17. What's the best way to count cows?
With a cow-culator.

18. What do you get if you cross a whale with a nun?
Blubber and sister.

19. What's the most popular game in a convent?
Nuntendo.

20. What is a mouse's least favourite newspaper?
Mews of the World.

21. Why did the cleaning woman stop cleaning?
She found that grime doesn't pay.

22. Why did the thief take a bath?
So he could make a clean getaway.

23. Who designed the first raincoat?
Anna Rack.

24. What's the difference between an Indian elephant and an African elephant?
About 3,000 miles.

25. What did the hotel manager say to the elephant who couldn't pay his bill?
'Pack your trunk and get out.'

26. What do you get if you cross an elephant with a goldfish?
Swimming trunks.

27. What do you call a
    woman with two toilets?
Lulu.

28. What do short-sighted
    ghosts wear?
Spook-tacles.

29. How do ghosts get through a locked
    door?
They have a skeleton key.

30. What do his victims call Dracula?
A pain in the neck.

31. What's Dracula's favourite song?
'Fangs for the Memory.'

32. Where does Dracula get all his jokes?
From his cryptwriter.

33. 'Doctor, Doctor – everyone thinks I'm
    a liar.'
'I don't believe you.'

34. 'Doctor, Doctor – I keep thinking I'm invisible.'
'*Who said that?*'

35. What's small, white and smells?
A pong-pong ball.

36. What part of a fish weighs the most?
The scales.

1837: Victoria becomes Queen of England
What do you get if you cross a famous monarch with too many sweets?
Queen Sick-toria.

38. What do you get if you cross a famous monarch with a magician?
Queen Trick-toria.

39. Who invented fire?
Oh, some bright spark.

40. Who invented the four-day week?
Robinson Crusoe. He had all his work done by Friday.

41. What happened to the cat who swallowed a ball of wool?
She had mittens.

42. What's green, lives in a field and has 5000 legs?
Grass – I lied about the legs.

43. JACK: 'My dad plays the piano by ear.'
JILL: 'Mine plays it with his fingers.'
JOHN: 'Well, my dad fiddles with his whiskers!'

44. MUM: 'I've changed my mind.'
DAD: 'Is your new one any better?'

45. What is never seen but often changed?
Your mind.

46. How can you tell which end of a worm is his head?
Tickle him in the middle and see which end smiles.

47. DAD: 'How long do you think a man can live without a brain?'
MUM: 'I don't know – how old are you again?'

48. HARRY: 'I've just found this wig in the street.'
POLICEMAN: 'You'd better take it to a psychiatrist. It's obviously off its head.'

49. What do you get if you cross a chicken with a cement mixer?
A bricklayer.

50. What do you get if you cross a carrier pigeon with a woodpecker?
A bird that knocks before he delivers his message.

51. HANDY ANDY: 'I've come to repair your doorbell, madam.'

WOMAN: 'You should have come yesterday!'

HANDY ANDY: 'I did – I rang the bell five times but nobody answered!'

52. MAN: 'How do I get to the hospital from here?'

POLICEMAN: 'Stand in the middle of that road for a few seconds.'

53. MR ANGRY: 'I'll teach you to throw stones at my greenhouse!'

NAUGHTY NICK: 'I wish you would, I've had ten shots and haven't hit it once.'

54. TEACHER: 'Give me a sentence with the word *centimetre* in it.'

ALI: 'My aunt was coming to visit us and I was centimetre.'

55. BRAINBOX: 'How did you find the exam questions?'

DIMWIT: 'The questions were all right, it was just the answers I had trouble with.'

56. TEACHER: 'If we breathe oxygen in the daytime, what do we breathe at night?'
EMILY: 'Nitrogen.'

57. What do you do if you find a blue banana?
Try and cheer it up.

58. Where would you find a stupid shoplifter?
Squashed under the shop.

59. What's the deadliest thing in the ocean?
Billy the Squid.

60. How does an octopus go into battle?
Well armed.

61. What grows up while it grows down?
A baby duckling.

62. JASMINE: 'My little brother's just
    fallen down a man-hole, what shall I
    do?'
ROSE: 'Run to the library and get a book
    on raising children.'

63. PETE: 'I passed your house yesterday.'
PAULINE: 'Thanks, I appreciate it.'

64. Did you hear the joke about the drill?
It's boring.

65. Why did the owl 'owl?
Because the woodpecker woodpecker.

66. A man goes into a butcher's shop and
    asks, 'Have you got a sheep's head?'
*The butcher says, 'No, it's just the way I
    part my hair.'*

67. What did one ear say to the other ear?
Between you and me, we need a haircut.

68. What tree grows near the seaside?
A beech tree.

69. What stars go to jail?
Shooting stars.

70. What do you give a sick bird?
Tweetment.

71. What dance do hippies hate?
A square dance.

72. What did the biscuit say when his friend was run over?
Crumbs!

73. Why is it so cheap to feed a giraffe?
A little goes a long way.

74. What lies on the ground a hundred
feet in the air?
A centipede lying on its back.

75. If a red house is made from red bricks
and a blue house is made from blue
bricks, what's a green house made
from?
Glass.

1876: The telephone is invented
What was more useful than the invention
   of the first telephone?
The invention of the second one.

77. What flowers grow under your nose?
Tulips.

78. What can you do if a herd of
   elephants come racing towards you?
   *Make a trunk call and reverse the
      charge.*

79. What's the difference between
   a nail and a bad boxer?
*One's knocked in, the other's
   knocked out.*

80. What's an elastic-band thief called?
A rubber bandit.

81. What goes *chuff-chuff* at a wedding?
The bride's train.

82. What is a caterpillar?
A worm in a fur coat.

83. What is a bee?
A little humbug.

84. 'What do misers do in cold weather?'
'Sit round a candle.'
'What do misers do in very cold weather?'
'Light it!'

85. Why do bees have sticky hair?
Because they have honey combs.

86. What's worse than being with a fool?
Fooling with a bee.

87. Who gets the sack every time he goes to work?
A postman.

88. Why did the lady have her hair in a bun?
Because she had her nose in a cheeseburger.

90. TEACHER: 'Can you say your name backwards?'
SIMON: 'No, Mis.'

90. Why is it useless to send a telegram to Washington these days?
Because he's dead.

91. Why couldn't the butterfly get into the dance?
Because it was a mothball.

92. Why did the egg sail across the world?
Because it was an eggsplorer.

93. How do you get a baby astronaut to sleep?
Rock-et.

94. What key in music makes a good army officer?
A sharp major.

95. Did you hear about the monster with pedestrian eyes?
They look both ways before they cross.

96. What did the baby skunk want to be when it grew up?
A big stinker.

97. Why was the horse hot-headed?
Because it had a blaze on its forehead.

98. How did the rich people get their money?
They stayed calm and collected.

99. Why is history the sweetest lesson at school?
Because it's full of dates.

100. What are two rows of cabbages called?
A dual cabbageway.

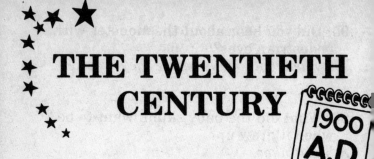

THE TWENTIETH CENTURY

1900 A.D.

1901: Queen Victoria dies
What did Queen Victoria say when she
  trod in a cowpat?
We are not a-moo-sed.

2. What do you do if you hear a guinea
  pig squeaking?
Oil it.

3. How are a dog and a penny alike?
Both have a head and a tail.

4. How long should your legs be?
Long enough to reach the ground.

5. When is an eye not an eye?
When the wind makes it water.

6. DAD: 'Did you get a haircut?'
MUM: 'No, I got all of them cut.'

7. SID: 'My brother was arrested for
   having flat feet.'
SINDY: 'Why's that?'
SID: 'They were in the wrong flat.'

8. What do you call a woman with one leg
   shorter than the other?
Eileen.

9. Why did the jockey take hay to bed?
To feed his nightmare.

10. Why did the man take his pencil to
    bed?
He wanted to draw the curtains.

11. If six smoky sausages sizzled in a
    saucepan – how many *S*'s in that?
None – there are no S's in 'that'.

1912: The *Titanic* sinks

What do you get if you cross the Atlantic with the *Titanic*?

Halfway.

13: What else do you get if you cross the Atlantic with the *Titanic*?
Very wet.

14. PASSENGER ON THE *TITANIC*: 'How often do ships like this sink?'
CAPTAIN: 'Only once.'

15. How did the Egyptian baby get a cold?
It caught it from its mummy.

16. Why do elephants have corrugated feet?
To give mice a fifty-fifty chance.

17. What would happen if everyone had a pink car?
We'd be a pink car nation.

18. What did Dracula say as he bit into
    Santa's neck?
'This is really going to sleigh you!'

19. What goes *putt, putt, putt*?
A bad golfer.

20. And what goes *oom, oom*?
A cow walking backwards.

21. What's brown and sticky?
A stick.

22. What happened to the idiot who
    listened to the match?
He burned his ear.

23. Why are brides unlucky?
They never marry the best man.

24. Which bird always succeeds?
A budgie with no teeth.

25. What is pink, wobbly and flies?
A jellycopter.

26. What goes *croak! croak!* when it's misty?
A froghorn.

27. What does a buffalo say when leaving his young son alone?
'Bison.'

28. What's big, grey and mutters?
A mumbo-jumbo.

29. What do you give an elephant with big feet?
Plenty of room.

30. Did you hear about the man who crossed an electric blanket with a toaster?
He kept popping out of bed all night.

31. What do you flatten a ghost with?
A spirit level.

32. Why does a witch ride on a broomstick?
A vacuum cleaner is too heavy.

33. What do you call a wicked old woman
who lives by the sea?
A sand-witch.

34. What did the boy octopus say to the
girl octopus?
*'I want to hold your hand hand hand
hand hand hand hand hand.'*

34. How do you help a deaf fisherman?
Give him a herring aid.

36. What do sea monsters eat?
Fish and ships.

37. What's the best way to communicate
with a fish?
Drop it a line.

38. Why is the theatre such a sad place?
Because the seats are always in tiers.

39. Where do fish wash?
In a river basin.

40. What's small, blue and furry?
A mouse holding its breath.

41. Why did the man throw his clock out
of the window?
He wanted to see time fly.

42. Why does lightning shock people?
It doesn't know how to conduct itself.

43. When is a car not a car?
When it turns into a street.

44. What letter is a vegetable?
The letter P.

45. What's green and holds up
   stagecoaches?
Dick Gherkin.

46. Why shouldn't you tell secrets in a
   vegetable garden?
*Because potatoes have eyes, corn has ears
   and beans talk.*

47. Why wouldn't the little boy eat an
   apple?
Because his gran had died of apple-plexy.

1948: Prince Charles is born
Why is Prince Charles like part of the
   postal service?
Because he is a royal male.

49. Why did the farmer call his rooster Robinson?
Because it crew so.

50. Why do birds fly south in winter?
It's too far to walk.

51. What's the fastest vegetable?
A runner bean.

52. Why is it silly to hold a party for a chicken?
Because these days it's difficult to make hens meet.

53. JOE: 'I once had a parrot for five years and it never said a word.'
MO: 'What a shame!'
JOE: 'Not really, it was stuffed.'

54. 'Doctor, Doctor – I keep stealing things.'
'Have you taken anything for it?'

55. What's the difference between a burglar and a man wearing a wig?
One has false keys, the other has false locks.

56. What's a good way to waste time?
Try telling a bald man hair-raising stories.

57. What man do you always take your hat off to?
The barber.

58. How do we know that Moses wore a wig?
Because he was sometimes seen with Aaron, and sometimes without.

59. What did the hat say to the scarf?
'You hang around, I'll go on ahead.'

60. 'Would you like to buy a pocket calculator, sir?'
'No thanks, I know how many pockets I've got.'

61. PIANO TUNER: 'I've come to tune your piano.'
MAN: 'But we didn't send for you!'
PIANO TUNER: 'I know, but your neighbours did.'

62. Did you hear about the musician who spent all his time in bed?
He wrote sheet music.

63. How do you make gold soup?
Put fourteen carrots in it.

64. What did the rake say to the hoe?
Hi, hoe!

65. MUM: 'Don't you have any friends to play with?'
MEL: 'Oh, I have friends, but I hate them.'

66. Why did the chicken walk over the hill?
Because it couldn't walk under it.

67. Why do people laugh up their sleeves?
Because that's where their funny bone is.

68. MUM: 'Angela, pick your feet up when you walk!'
ANGELA: 'But Mum, I'll only have to put them down again.'

1969: Neil Armstrong is the first man to walk on the moon
What do spacemen play in their spare time?
Astronoughts and crosses.

70. What's mad and goes to the moon?
A loony module.

71. What do you get if you cross a dog
    with *Concorde*?
A jet-setter.

72. SPARROW: 'Look, there's *Concorde* – I
    wish I could fly like that.'
BLACKBIRD: 'You could if your bottom was
    on fire.'

73. What are long, pointed and run in
    families?
Noses.

74. What jacket is always burning?
A blazer.

75. Why did the fly fly?
*Because the spider
    spied 'er.*

76. What did the dirt
    say to the rain?
*'If this keeps up, my
    name'll be mud.'*

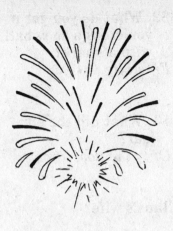

77. Why do ghosts like to haunt tall buildings?
Because there are lots of scarecases.

78. What's short, green and goes camping?
A boy sprout.

79. What relation is a doorstep to a doormat?
A step farther.

80. What's bread?
Raw toast.

81. What goes over the water, under the water, on the water and yet never touches the water?
An egg in a duck's tummy.

82. What do you get if
    you cross a snowball
    with a shark?
Frostbite.

83. What did the ear
    'ear?
Only the nose knows.

84. Who is Santa Claus's wife?
Mary Christmas.

85. What's the most bad-tempered
    pudding?
Apple grumble.

86. What cake gives you an
    electric shock?
A currant bun.

87. DOCTOR: 'How did you get
    here so fast?'
PATIENT: 'Flu.'

88. How many wives does a man have
    when he gets married?
*Four better, four worse, four richer, four
    poorer.*

89. BAD BILL: 'Give me all your money or
    I'll shoot you.'
DIM JIM: 'Shoot me – I need my money for
    when I'm old.'

90. What is rhubarb?
*Celery with high blood
    pressure.*

91. What happens when two French
    prams collide?
You have a crèche.

92. What do you get if you cross a donkey
    with a mother?
Ass-ma.

93. What do bees do with their honey?
Cell it.

94. Where can you always find money if you need it?
In the dictionary.

95. Old refrigerators never die.
They just lose their cool.

96. What do you do if you lock yourself out of the house?
Keep singing till you find the right key.

97. What turns without moving?
Milk. It turns sour.

98. What's the first thing that the Queen does in the morning?
Wakes up.

99. What do you call a little man who
  lives in Greenwich?
The Millennium Gnome.

2000: A new millennium begins . . .
What do you get if you cross a beetle with
  the year 2000?
A millennium bug.

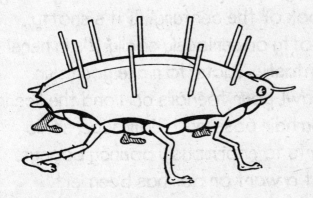

BOGEYS, BOILS & BELLY BUTTONS

JIM AND DUNCAN ELDRIDGE

Fancy dipping into the most disgusting book of the century? If it's snotty, spotty or seriously smelly, it's in here! Fantastic 'facts' to make your skin crawl, your toenails curl and the lice in you hair pass out! From supersonic farts to enormously bouncy bogeys, not a wart or boil has been left uncharted in our quest to find the most gruesomely gross exhibits in the history of all things putrid and pukey...!

WARNING

THIS BOOK CAN SERIOUSLY UPSET YOUR STOMACH.

ISBN 0 09 944750 9   £2.99

FROM CHRISTMAS CRACK-UPS TO EGG-
CELLANT EGG JOKES, THEY'RE ALL HERE IN
THE RED FOX JOKE BOOKS!

SANTA'S CHRISTMAS JOKE BOOK

Katie Wales

You'll be giggling over your turkey
and groaning under the mistletoe with
this crazy collection of Christmas corkers!

ISBN 0 09 926703 9   £2.99

THE GOOD EGG YOLK BOOK

Katie Wales

Eggs-actly what you need
to become an
eggs-pert joker!

It'll crack you up!

ISBN 0 09 965960 3   £2.99

TAKE A DEEP BREATH AND REACH FOR
THE SMELLING SALTS BEFORE ENTERING THE
RED FOX JOKE ZONE - HOME OF THE
SMELLIEST JOKES AROUND!

THE SMELLY SOCKS JOKE BOOK

Susan Abbott

Packed with pungent puns and reeking with
revolting riddles, it's guaranteed to leave you
gasping for air!

ISBN 0 09 9562707   £2.99

THE EVEN SMELLIER SOCKS JOKE BOOK

Karen King

The pongiest and most putrid collection of
gagtastic gags you'll ever come across.
Guaranteed to make you laugh till you hurl!

ISBN 0 09 926513 3   £2.99

WARNING: THEY STINK!